WOMEN AND CHILDREN FIRST

SINKING OF THE TITANIC

Virginia Loh-Hagan

45th Parallel Press

Published in the United States of America by Cherry Lake Publishing
Ann Arbor, Michigan
www.cherrylakepublishing.com

Reading Adviser: Marla Conn MS, Ed., Literacy specialist, Read-Ability, Inc.
Book Designer: Felicia Macheske

Photo Credits: © ILYA AKINSHIN/Shutterstock.com, cover, 1; © mdbildes/Shutterstock.com, cover, 1; Bain Collection, Library of Congress, LC-USZ62-26743, 5; © Maksym Gorpenyuk/Shutterstock.com, 6; © Everett Historical/Shutterstock.com, 11, 12, 23; © Anton_Ivanov/Shutterstock.com, 17; © S.Bachstroem/Shutterstock.com, 18; © Denis Burdin/Shutterstock.com, 21; Library of Congress, LC-USZ62-116257, 25; Bain Collection, Library of Congress, LC-DIG-ggbain-10384, 29

Graphic Elements Throughout: © Chipmunk131/Shutterstock.com; © Nowik Sylwia/Shutterstock.com;
© Andrey_Popov/Shutterstock.com; © NadzeyaShanchuk/Shutterstock.com; © KathyGold/Shutterstock.com;
© Black creator/Shutterstock.com; © Edvard Molnar/Shutterstock.com; © Elenadesign/Shutterstock.com;
© estherpoon/Shutterstock.com

45th Parallel Press is an imprint of Cherry Lake Publishing.

Library of Congress Cataloging-in-Publication Data has been filed and is available at catalog.loc.gov

Cherry Lake Publishing would like to acknowledge the work of The Partnership for 21st Century Skills.
Please visit www.p21.org for more information.

Printed in the United States of America
Corporate Graphics

A Note on Dramatic Retellings

Participating in Readers Theater, or dramatic retellings, can greatly improve reading skills, especially fluency. The books in the **BEHIND THE CURTAIN** series give readers opportunities to learn about important historical events in a fun and engaging way. These books serve as a bridge to more complex texts. All the characters are real figures from history; however, their stories have been fictionalized. To learn more about the people and the events, check out the Viewpoints and Perspectives series and the Perspectives Library series, as the **BEHIND THE CURTAIN** books are aligned to these stories.

TABLE of CONTENTS

HISTORICAL BACKGROUND 4

CAST OF CHARACTERS 8

ACT 1 10

ACT 2 20

EVENT TIMELINE 30

Consider This! 31

Learn More 31

Index 32

About the Author 32

HISTORICAL BACKGROUND

The *Titanic* is the world's most famous ship. When it was built, it was the world's largest ship. It was big. It was fancy. It was beautiful. It was supposed to be "unsinkable." But it hit an iceberg. This happened on April 14, 1912. Over 2 hours later, the *Titanic* sank. There were only 705 survivors.

The *Titanic* set sail on April 10, 1912. This was its maiden voyage. It left England. It was going to New York. There were over 2,200 passengers on board. Over 1,500 people died. It's one of the deadliest sea disasters in history.

FLASH FACT!
The Titanic *was built in Ireland.*

Vocabulary

unsinkable (un-SINGK-uh-buhl) not having the ability to sink

iceberg (ISE-burg) a big, floating chunk of ice

survivors (sur-VYE-vurz) people who live through something bad

maiden voyage (MAY-duhn VOI-ij) the first trip

passengers (PAS-uhn-jurz) people traveling

Vocabulary
crew (KROO) workers
flooded (FLUHD-id) filled with water
rescued (RES-kyood) saved

The ship received several warnings of ice. But the warnings didn't get to the captain. A member of the crew saw the iceberg. But it was too late. The ship couldn't turn quickly enough. The iceberg cut open the ship's side. Water flooded the ship.

The captain gave orders to load the lifeboats. But there weren't enough lifeboats. The lifeboats also weren't filled all the way. Not everyone was able to get away. People on the ship sank with the ship. People who jumped off drowned in the cold, icy water. The captain went down with the ship.

The *Carpathia* rescued survivors. It picked people up. It brought people to land.

CAST of CHARACTERS

NARRATOR: person who helps tell the story

MAGGIE DONAVAN: passenger traveling **third class** with her parents and younger brothers

RHODA ABBOTT: third-class passenger, English woman who was moving to the United States, mother of two sons, **seamstress**

EVA HART: passenger, young girl traveling **second class** with her parents

JACOB ASTOR: passenger traveling **first class**, richest person on the ship, businessman, husband

LUCY WINN-NORTON: first-class passenger, rich wife of Lord Peter Norton

WILLIAM DAVIES: crew member who's looking out for icebergs

BACKSTORY
SPOTLIGHT BIOGRAPHY

Joseph Laroche lived from 1886 to 1912. He was born in Haiti. He was one of the few black people on the *Titanic*. At age 15, he studied in France. He got an engineering degree. He married a French woman named Juliette Lafargue. He had two daughters. He couldn't find work due to the color of his skin. In 1912, Juliette found out she was pregnant. This was their third child. Laroche wanted to return to Haiti. So, he got tickets on the *Titanic*. He and his family boarded as second-class passengers. The ship hit the iceberg. Laroche woke up his family. He put his pregnant wife and two daughters on a lifeboat. His family survived. But he did not. He died with the ship. His body was never found. His family returned to France. The baby was named Joseph.

Vocabulary

third class (THURD KLAS) also known as steerage, the cheapest way to travel

seamstress (SEEM-stris) a person who sews clothes

second class (SEK-uhnd KLAS) the way to travel for the middle class

first class (FURST KLAS) the most expensive and fanciest way to travel

FLASH FACT!

Margaret Tobin Brown is called the "unsinkable Molly Brown." She was a survivor. She wanted her lifeboat to find more survivors.

ACT 1

NARRATOR: *It's April 10, 1912. People have just boarded the* Titanic. **MAGGIE DONAVAN** *and* **RHODA ABBOTT** *are on the third-class* **deck***.*

MAGGIE: This ship is so fancy!

RHODA: If you think third class is fancy, you should see first class. Those people live like kings and queens.

MAGGIE: Let's go to the first-class deck!

RHODA: We're not allowed. First-class passengers paid a lot of money.

MAGGIE: It took my parents many years to pay for our tickets. We're going to start a new life in America.

RHODA: Same here. I bought tickets for me and my two sons. I had to work many late hours to save up. Our **cabins** are so low in the ship. I can hear the ship's machines. But it's better than other ships. At least we have our own cabins. On other ships, third-class passengers sleep in one big room.

Vocabulary
deck (DEK) outside area
cabins (KAB-inz) rooms on a ship

FLASH FACT!
Third-class cabins on the Titanic *were the best of the time, but still small compared to first- and second-class living.*

MAGGIE: I'm happy with my small **bunk**. I don't care about being in **steerage**. I'm on the biggest and fanciest ship in the world!

RHODA: My sons are happy too. There's plenty to do here. People dance. They sing. It's like a big party.

NARRATOR: MAGGIE DONAVAN *explores the ship. She runs into* EVA HART.

MAGGIE: Is this first class?

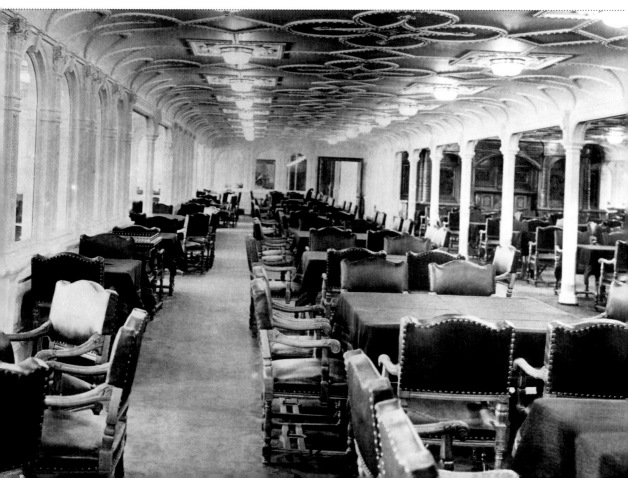

EVA: This is second class. My father has a small business. We're not rich enough for first class.

MAGGIE: But it's so fancy here. You even have your own library!

EVA: It's pretty nice. But we were supposed to have first-class tickets on another ship.

MAGGIE: What happened?

EVA: That ship didn't have enough coal. So, we got tickets for the *Titanic*. My father is happy about it. He said everyone is talking about this ship.

Vocabulary
bunk (BUHNGK) bed
steerage (STEER-ij) the area closest to the bottom of the ship

FLASH FACT!
The last supper served to the first-class passengers consisted of 11 courses.

MAGGIE: This ship is unsinkable!

EVA: Don't say that around my mother! She has a bad feeling. She thinks we're **jinxing** ourselves.

MAGGIE: We'll be in New York in one week. What could go wrong in one week? This ship is strong and fast.

EVA: You're right. I do like the food here.

MAGGIE: Me too! They even serve ice cream!

NARRATOR: *JACOB ASTOR and LUCY WINN-NORTON are in first class. They're talking on the deck.*

JACOB: What brings you on board?

LUCY: Lord Norton and I are looking for a bit of adventure. We thought it would be **grand** to sail in style. What about you?

JACOB: My new wife and I were on vacation. She's **pregnant**. So, it's time to go back to New York. Plus, I want to see how this ship works. I've heard so much about it. What a **feat**!

LOCATION SHOOTING
REAL-WORLD SETTING

The *Titanic* sank to the seafloor. Its wreckage is 12,500 feet (3,810 meters) below the sea. The ship broke in two. The two parts are 1,970 feet (600 m) apart. The wreckage is 400 miles (644 kilometers) off the coast of Newfoundland. Newfoundland is the closest island to the *Titanic* wreckage. It's a part of Canada. It's in the Atlantic Ocean. It's the world's 16th-largest island. It's off the east coast of North America. It's a great place to look at icebergs. It has its own time zone. It's 90 minutes ahead of Eastern Time. Its capital is St. John's. St. John's is the oldest city in North America. It's been burnt down by fires. This has happened five times. The city's houses are painted in different colors. This is so ships can see them in the fog.

Vocabulary

jinxing (JINGKS-ing) bringing bad luck, tempting fate

grand (GRAND) great, fine

pregnant (PREG-nuhnt) having a baby growing inside

feat (FEET) a major accomplishment

FLASH FACT!
The grand staircase went down seven of the ship's decks. It showed the ship's luxury.

LUCY: How do you like the ship so far?

JACOB: It's been great. I'm looking forward to using the **gymnasium**. I'm also going to use the swimming pool. And, of course, I'll chat with our friends in the **smoking room**. How about you?

LUCY: It's just like home! We even have our own **servants**. Our **stateroom** is nicer than rooms at fancy hotels. We have a sitting room. We have a bedroom. We have a dressing room. We have our own bathroom.

JACOB: There's even a telephone on our deck!

LUCY: And our own musicians. I can't wait for tonight's **concerts**. This is the best ship I've ever been on!

Vocabulary

gymnasium (jim-NAY-zee-uhm)
a place to exercise

smoking room (SMOHK-ing ROOM)
a room for gentlemen to smoke and talk

servants (SUR-vuhnts)
people who serve

stateroom (STATE-room) a private apartment on a ship

concerts (KAHN-surts)
music shows

FLASH FACT!
The first-class passengers had many special features.

NARRATOR: *It's April 14, 1912. It's just after 11:30 p.m.* WILLIAM DAVIES *is on watch* **duty***. He's in the* **crow's nest***.* JACOB ASTOR *is on his nightly walk.*

JACOB: What are you doing up there?

WILLIAM: I'm the **lookout** tonight. I'm scanning the sea in front of the ship. I'm looking for anything in our way.

JACOB: That's good. I hear there are a lot of icebergs in this area.

WILLIAM: Yes, sir. We don't want to slow the ship. So, we have to keep a careful watch.

JACOB: It sure is cold.

WILLIAM: Yes, sir. It's one of the coldest nights of the year. The water is a little above freezing.

JACOB: Keep up the good work. Hopefully, nothing happens—

WILLIAM: Oh no! I think I see something! What do you think that is?

JACOB: It's too dark. I can't see anything.

WILLIAM: It's an iceberg! It's about 1,500 feet (457 m) away. I have to ring the warning bell. I have to tell the captain! Iceberg right ahead!

Vocabulary
duty (DOO-tee) job
crow's nest (KROHZ NEST) a little room high on a ship's mast
lookout (LUK-out) the person in charge of watching the waters ahead

FLASH FACT!
The iceberg was spotted from the crow's nest. The crow's nest is near the front of the ship.

ACT 2

NARRATOR: *An iceberg hits the* Titanic *at 11:40 p.m. on April 14, 1912. Passengers feel a rumble.* **JACOB ASTOR** *heads to his cabin. He runs into* **LUCY WINN-NORTON** *when she comes out of her cabin.*

LUCY: What was that?

JACOB: An iceberg hit us. It looked to be over 100 feet (30 m) high. I saw chunks of ice fall on the deck.

LUCY: The ship's **engines** have stopped. Should we worry?

JACOB: This ship is unsinkable. It'll be fine. I'm going to get my wife. I'll take her to the gymnasium. We'll be safer there. We'll wait for the **panic** to stop.

NARRATOR: EVA HART *is on deck. She's waiting to get into a lifeboat with her mother.* **WILLIAM DAVIES** *is helping the passengers.*

EVA: Did we really get hit by an iceberg? What happened?

WILLIAM: Yes, we did. The iceberg ripped a hole in the ship's side. We couldn't close the doors in time. Water came in.

Vocabulary

engines (EN-jinz) machines that make ships work

panic (PAN-ik) wild behavior caused by fear

FLASH FACT!

There were about 3,500 life jackets on the ship. However, they didn't keep people from freezing to death.

EVA: But I thought the ship was unsinkable?

WILLIAM: It was built to have four flooded rooms. But there are five or six flooded rooms. The ship can't handle that. Get in! Make **haste**!

EVA: What about my father?

WILLIAM: Women and children first. The men will join later. There's not much time. You have to get in.

NARRATOR: *Eva and her mother get into the lifeboat.* **WILLIAM DAVIES** *continues to help other people. He sees* **RHODA ABBOTT***.*

WILLIAM: Take my hand. I'll help you get in.

RHODA: Not without my sons.

WILLIAM: They can come with you. This is one of the last lifeboats.

Vocabulary
haste (HAYST) quickness

FLASH FACT!

Wooden lifeboats could hold 65 passengers, but the first one was launched with only 28 people in it.

RHODA: There are still over 1,000 people left!

WILLIAM: Every man for himself.

RHODA: Oh no! The ship just broke in two!

NARRATOR: RHODA ABBOTT *and her sons lose their step. They fall into the water.* **WILLIAM DAVIES** *also falls in.*

RHODA: Where are my sons? Where are they?

WILLIAM: Don't panic! I'll help you look.

RHODA: The water is so cold. They won't survive this!

Vocabulary
corpse (KORPS) dead body

FLASH FACT!
Newspapers around the world wrote about the ship's sinking.

WILLIAM: I can't find them. We have to get on that lifeboat.

RHODA: I can't leave my sons!

NARRATOR: *Rhoda Abbott was pulled into a lifeboat. She passed out. When she woke up, she learned her sons had died. They found one son's* **corpse**. *The other son's corpse was never found.*

NARRATOR: LUCY WINN-NORTON *and* EVA HART *are on the same lifeboat. They're waiting to be rescued by the* Carpathia.

LUCY: It's hard to row. This boat is too full. There are too many people in it.

EVA: The more lives we can save, the better. Look at all those empty seats in those other lifeboats. Such a shame!

LUCY: You're right. But we need to row better and faster. We have to get away from the ship. We don't want to get pulled under.

EVA: Oh no, your pretty dress. It's **ruined**! You must be from first class.

LUCY: I don't care about this dress. And classes don't matter now. We're all in the same boat. We've lost loved ones tonight.

EVA: My pa was on the ship.

LUCY: So was my dear husband.

BLOOPERS
HISTORICAL MISTAKES

The *Californian* was the closest ship to the *Titanic*. It was about 19 miles (30.6 km) away. It had stopped for the night. It saw the *Titanic*'s distress rockets. Distress means in need of help. Stanley Lord was the captain of the *Californian*. He ignored the rockets. He thought they were party lights. The ship's radio was turned off. No one heard the distress calls from the *Titanic*. Lord didn't do anything. The ship could've saved many lives. Lord finally heard about the disaster. He went to search for survivors. But he was too late. He just found ship pieces, empty lifeboats, and dead bodies. U.S. and British officials investigated. They said Lord's inaction was "reprehensible." This means shameful. Lord and his crew weren't punished. But people were upset. Lord became very unpopular. The *Californian* was later sunk. It sunk in 1915. A German submarine hit it. This happened during World War I.

Vocabulary
ruined (ROO-ind) destroyed

FLASH FACT!
The Carpathia *crew tried to keep the survivors warm.*

EVA: What happened to your friend, Mr. Astor?

LUCY: Poor Mr. Astor! He put his wife on a lifeboat. Some say he gave up his seat for women and children. I didn't see him get into a lifeboat. He probably died with the ship.

EVA: I don't know how much longer we can last. It's freezing. We're not dressed for this weather.

LUCY: I see the ship! I see the *Carpathia*. This ship is dropping rope ladders. We need to climb the ladders up to the ship.

EVA: I might slip through the **gaps**.

LUCY: Crew members are wrapping children in **sacks**. They're pulling them up.

EVA: We're saved!

NARRATOR: *Many people died. About 24 percent of third-class passengers survived. About 42 percent of second-class passengers survived. About 61 percent of first-class passengers survived.*

Vocabulary
gaps (GAPS) holes or spaces in between

sacks (SAKS) bags

FLASH FACT!

Jacob Astor's funeral was on May 4, 1912.

EVENT TIMELINE

July 1908: The design for the *Titanic* is approved.

March 31, 1909: The building of the *Titanic* begins. It's built in Ireland.

April 2, 1912: The *Titanic* leaves dock. It's tested for speed. It's tested for turns. It's tested for emergency stops. It heads for Southhampton, England.

April 3–10, 1912: The *Titanic* is loaded with supplies. Workers are hired.

April 10, 1912: Passengers board the *Titanic*. The ship leaves the dock at noon. Its first stop is France. Its second stop is Queenstown, Ireland.

April 11, 1912: The *Titanic* travels across the Atlantic Ocean. It heads for New York.

April 14, 1912: The *Titanic* gets warnings about icebergs. These messages never get to the captain. The ship hits an iceberg.

April 15, 1912: The *Titanic* begins to sink. People get into lifeboats. The ship snaps in half. It sinks at 2:20 a.m. The *Carpathia* is about 58 miles (93 km) away from the *Titanic*. This ship helps rescue people.

April 17, 1912: The *Mackay-Bennett* is a ship. It travels to the crash site. It's the first of several ships to search for bodies.

April 18, 1912: The *Carpathia* arrives in New York. There are 705 survivors.

April 19–May 25, 1912: The U.S. government investigates the disaster. They ask questions about the number of lifeboats.

May 2–July 3, 1912: British officials investigate the disaster.

September 1, 1985: Robert Ballard is a sea explorer. He finds the wreckage of the *Titanic*.

CONSIDER THIS!

TAKE A POSITION! Some people think the *Titanic* wreckage should be a memorial. They think people should leave it alone. This is to honor the people who died on the ship. Other people want to study it. They want to tour it. What do you think? Should it be a memorial? Or should it be a public attraction? Argue your point with reasons and evidence.

SAY WHAT? Read the 45th Parallel Press book about Violet Jessop. Explain how she's connected to the *Titanic*. Explain the significance of her story. How would you add her story to this *Behind the Curtain* series?

THINK ABOUT IT! People love the story of the *Titanic*. There are movies about it. There are books about it. Why do people love it? Why is it so interesting? Why are you interested in it?

LEARN MORE

Hopkinson, Deborah. *Titanic: Voices from the Disaster*. New York: Scholastic Paperbacks, 2014

Lusted, Marcia Amidon. *The Sinking of the Titanic*. Ann Arbor, MI: Cherry Lake Publishing, 2014.

Russo, Kristin J. *Viewpoints on the Sinking of the Titanic*. Ann Arbor, MI: Cherry Lake Publishing, 2019.

Sabol, Stephanie. *What Was the Titanic?* New York: Penguin, 2018.

INDEX

Abbott, Rhoda, 8, 10–12, 22, 24–25

Astor, Jacob, 8, 14, 16, 18–19, 20, 28, 29

Brown, Margaret Tobin, 9

Californian, 27
Carpathia, 7, 26, 27, 28

Davies, William, 8, 18–19, 21–22, 24–25
Donavan, Maggie, 8, 10–14

first-class passengers, 8, 10, 13, 14, 16, 26, 28

Hart, Eva, 8, 12–14, 21–22, 26, 28

iceberg, 4, 6, 7, 8, 9, 15, 18–21

Laroche, Joseph, 9
life jackets, 21
lifeboats, 7, 22, 23, 25, 28
Lord, Stanley, 27

Newfoundland, 15

second-class passengers, 8, 9, 13, 28
steerage, 12
survivors, 4, 7, 27, 28

third-class passengers, 8, 10–11, 28
Titanic, 4, 5
distress calls, 27
timeline, 30
wreckage, 15

"unsinkable Molly Brown," 9

Winn-Norton, Lucy, 8, 14, 16, 20, 26, 28

ABOUT THE AUTHOR

Dr. Virginia Loh-Hagan is an author, university professor, and former classroom teacher. She can play "My Heart Will Go On" on the piano. She lives in San Diego with her very tall husband and very naughty dogs. To learn more about her, visit www.virginialoh.com.